POSITIVE ATTITUDE HANDBOOK

Five Easy Steps to
More Positive Thinking in
Five Minutes a Day

BY MAXINE SWISA

Dear Jeremy
Thank you for your warm
welcome and wonderful hugs!

All the best.
love,
Maxine Swisa

POSITIVE ATTITUDE HANDBOOK

Copyright © 2013 by Maxine Swisa

All rights reserved. No part of this publication
may be reproduced, stored in a retrieval system,
or transmitted by any means – electronic,
mechanical, photographic (photocopying),
recording, or otherwise – without prior
permission in writing from the author.

Printed in the United States of America
ISBN: 0989366200
ISBN 13: 9780989366205
Library of Congress Control Number: 2013939817
Green Back Publishing Santa Fe NEW MEXICO

Learn more at:
www.greenbackpublishing.com

**Ten percent of all profits from this
book will be donated to the nonprofit
Unicopia, www.unicopia.org, a public
benefit company dedicated to cultivating
the awareness, knowledge, and synergy
essential to our sustainable future.**

This book is lovingly dedicated to the memories of my mother, Lucille Okoshkin, and my sister, Judith Okoshkin Lubiner, both of whom embodied eternal optimism.

ACKNOWLEDGMENTS

We all have people who make our days fuller and our lives happier. I would like to thank some of my closest friends and family who have supported me and encouraged me while writing this book.

Maya and Adi Swisa, my beautiful and talented daughters, who are blossoming into amazing women and have taught me everything I know about unconditional love.

Sara Novenson, a talented artist and great friend, with whom I have shared joy and sorrow. She has guided me on a spiritual path that has led me to write this book.

Faren Dancer, my friend and business partner, whose vision for a more sustainable future has enriched my life immensely.

Jenny Lake Sanborn, who, by her very nature, is a positive and encouraging friend and colleague.

Darla Sather, my dear friend, who has been there for me through thick and thin.

Madelyn Krassner, my hiking buddy, whose strength and courage inspire me.

Joan Miller, my oldest friend and beach buddy, with whom I have shared a lifetime of memories, and spent countless hours shooting the breeze while listening to the waves and lounging at the beach.

Jamie Goodman, my cousin, who taught me the importance of mindfulness.

Phyllis Wolf, my sister, who reminds me of the preciousness of family. I am forever grateful to her for introducing me to The Beatles on *The Ed Sullivan Show* in 1964!

To my friends and family, all of whom are on their own spiritual journey: Thank you for always being there for me.

TABLE OF CONTENTS

STUDENT OF LIFE

Life is full of lessons. Some lessons are more pleasant than others. Do you believe that things happen for a reason? If you do, then it is important to remember that bumps in the road are opportunities to learn and grow. When we understand this, we are able to learn something from all of our experiences, even the difficult ones. These opportunities ultimately make us stronger and wiser. This approach is what I call a hope-based view of life. When we live from a hope-based view of life, we look for options and choices when challenges arise. We feel empowered. Hope is a positive emotion that offers expansive possibilities.

For many of us, it is often easier to notice what is wrong, rather than what is right, in our lives and the world. After all, we are surrounded by bad news everywhere we look: on TV, in the newspaper, on the Internet. It often feels as if we live in a pessimistic world. The information disseminated in this manner is fear-based. Fear is a negative emotion that constricts us.

It doesn't have to be that way. I have learned that it feels much more empowering to operate from a hope-based approach to life. It is almost always possible to turn lemons into lemonade (even if it doesn't immediately feel that way). People do it all the time. Life is full of setbacks and obstacles as well as rewards and gifts.

I had several setbacks during these past few years. My marriage ended. I worked at a highly stressful job and decided to retire early. Shortly after I retired, the Great Recession began, which disrupted my dreams of financial security. The hardest setbacks of all were the losses of my sister and my mother within a seven-month period. It would have been easy for me to remain in a state of despair. I was surrounded by even more reasons to be pessimistic: One of my closest friends struggled with health issues, and many others struggled with family issues, relationship issues, and financial issues.

In spite of these challenges, I continued to look for moments of gratitude and transformation. I expanded my spiritual practice. I partnered with Faren Dancer, a designer, builder, and thought leader, to create the award-winning zero-energy Emerald Home in Santa Fe, New Mexico. I became an ESOL (English for Speakers of Other Languages) teacher and a certified Laughter Yoga facilitator. Faren and I re-energized a nonprofit, Unicopia, www.unicopia.org, which is founded on the principles of unity consciousness and prosperity. Once we realize that all life is interconnected and that we have the power to heal the planet and ourselves, we can then create a community of abundance, love, joy, and peace. (Ten percent of all profits from this book will be donated to Unicopia.)

Even when we experience many wonderful things, we still need to remember to focus on feeling grateful. This book arose out of my desire to help others feel better, more positive, and more grateful, because out of these heart-opening intentions, love, compassion, and kindness arise.

The Five Easy Steps presented in this book offer a process that facilitates feeling better. Once you start feeling more positive, you will naturally begin to look for more positive news. There are many websites that provide remarkable stories involving acts of kindness and demonstrating goodness in the world. Share some of these good news stories. Read spiritual and uplifting books. Watch movies that show the many wonderful things people are doing to make the world a better place. Watch movies that make you laugh. Begin to write affirmations of gratitude.

I took this one step further and created a website and posted affirmations on it (www. gratefuloptimism.com). All of this has been a healing process and a wonderful reminder to me of all that is good in the world and in my life. We are fortunate to have so many inspiring resources at our fingertips. I have listed some of my favorites in the Resource Section at the back of the book, and this is just the beginning.

There are many books written about being positive and many more about meditation. Some of them may have the opposite effect and make you feel discouraged because they require a large time commitment from the outset. How many of us can start out by dedicating an hour a day, in the morning and the evening, to meditate? How many of us *want* to start out by dedicating an hour a day to this?

That always felt daunting to me. Eventually I would give up. It never quite jibed with my disposition. So I decided to follow the easy guidelines described in this book. It has made a remarkable difference in my life. I hope it does the same for you.

I wish you inner joy, greater peace of mind, glimpses of true mindfulness, and a more positive sense of well-being.

Enjoy!

CHAPTER ONE

BREATHE

If you remember only one thing from this book, let it be to **take a deep breath**. Before you continue reading, take a deep breath. Breath is the crux of human life. It is easy to take it for granted because most of us do it so automatically.

While you read, try to pay attention to your breath. Whenever you remember, take a deep breath or two or three or more. Does it feel good? If it does, do it often and enjoy!

As you breathe, observe your bodily sensations and your mental activity. How are you feeling physically and emotionally? Do you have any discomfort? Try to pay attention without judging…Simply be an observer to your process.

I will remind you repeatedly to take a deep breath as you read. Conscious breathing is the key to mindful living and awareness.

Go ahead, take a deep breath!

CHAPTER TWO

ENJOY THE RIDE

While you are reading, you will notice that I ask you a lot of questions in order to provide you with opportunities for self-reflection, self-awareness, and mindfulness.

I encourage you to record your thoughts and your process. If there is something that comes up that you want to remember, make a note of it.

RATE YOUR TYPICAL DAY.

How do you feel most days? On a scale of one to ten, rate your typical day. If you can rate it as a seven or higher, you're doing very well. Please feel free to share your positive attitude stories with others on my blog at gratefuloptimism.com.

Even if you are able to rate your typical day as a seven or higher, there's always room for improvement. This book will guide you through easy, manageable steps toward a more positive outlook on yourself, your relationships, and life.

THINK ABOUT YOUR TYPICAL DAY.

It starts by waking up. If you use an alarm clock, how does that feel? If it doesn't feel good, try training yourself to wake up without an alarm clock. Set your own internal clock. Before you go to bed, tell yourself the time you would like to wake up in the morning. It might take a few attempts, but see how long it takes until you are able to wake up on your own. You may be surprised to discover how easy it is.

OK, so you wake up, then what happens?
Do you lie in bed for a while?
Do you think about what you have to do once you get out of bed?

Do you have a sense of dread about work or another responsibility?

Do you feel apprehension about money?

Do you have a sense of fatigue before you even get started?

Are you thinking about your job?

Are you thinking about your family?

Are you thinking about your relationships?

Are your friends on your mind?

CHECK IN WITH YOURSELF.

Take a moment to think about these questions. How are you feeling right now? If you are like me, some of these questions bring up good feelings and others bring up not so good feelings.

A NEW WAY TO START EACH DAY.

What if you were able to start your day with a smile on your face before you even got out of bed? Well, I'm happy to tell you that you can. That is, if you really want to. That is the power of free will and mind over matter.

In this book, you will learn techniques that will help you greet each day with a more positive attitude and at least one thought of gratitude.

The challenge with a lot of routines is just that—they feel like routines, even if they are meant to be routines to help you feel better. For the moment, let's forget about routines and make this short, easy, and fun. You can stay in bed. You can keep your eyes closed. Just relax.

The only rules you need to follow are:

- **Keep it simple.**
- **Make sure it feels good.**
- **Take a deep breath.**
- **Focus on your breath.**

If anything you do while you read this book feels like a chore, reevaluate your approach and your attitude. What is it that seems difficult?

Please remember that these are meant as guidelines. Feel free to pick, choose, and modify.

Before I introduce the Five Easy Steps, think about why you purchased this book. Clearly, there was a reason. What was it? Keep that intention in mind as you read.

This book does not need to be read sequentially. At any point, feel free to review the Five Easy Steps and start making them a part of your daily routine. If you need a little more encouragement before you dive in, read the whole book or any part that naturally appeals to you. You can also do what I do: I turn to the Table of Contents and close my eyes. I point to something on the Table of Contents page and then open the book to that section. Usually there is a message in the section that I need to focus on. Think about the message. Why is it important to you at this moment? What do you need to pay attention to? Use the message as a point of contemplation.

Once again, take a deep breath. Remember to have fun and enjoy the ride.

CHAPTER THREE

HABITS

What is a habit? Dictionary.com defines a habit as an acquired behavior pattern. This is a good place to start. There have been books written about how to make something a habit. Many of these books include a specific number of days or times it takes to make something a habit. I have read that it can take anywhere from twenty-one to forty days. However, there is a challenge with putting a number to this process: The challenge is what I refer to as the "human factor." We are all unique individuals. What works for one person might not work for another individual. What might take one person three weeks to become a habit might take another person six weeks or longer. Our individual desires and motivations are ultimately what facilitate the habit-making process. We have to really *want* to make something stick. I know that for me personally, there have been times when I have made something a "habit" based on the forty-day rule, and when I stopped practicing, I didn't miss the integration of the "habit" in my daily life. What I realized is that the *desire* to make and keep something a habit becomes the ultimate decider in the long-term success or failure of a newly formed habit.

For the purpose of this book, the habit we want to form is to be more positive.

The first questions to ask are:

- Are you truly motivated? Why?
- What do you want to change in your life?
- Take a moment to think about this. Jot down some notes if you like.

Keep this in mind as you continue to read. If you want the steps outlined in this book to help you, they will. This is because you are *ready* and *willing* to make some changes. So much of our success in life is based on our attitude and motivation.

Ponder that before you continue. When you're sure you want to exchange some old, negative habits for some new, positive ones, please continue.

The five steps are the easy part. It's our mind that is the obstacle. So let's start by removing obstacles.

Do you tend to make excuses for why you can't do something? Or why you don't want to do something? We all have our own individual story that may block us from moving forward. What's your story? What holds you back from feeling joy?

More often than not, it requires an attitude adjustment. If we approach life with a positive, self-empowered attitude, we will naturally feel better about our lives. It's about changing our story. In order to change our story, we need to change habits.

A close friend was going through a divorce. Any of us who have been through that knows that the loss of that primary relationship sends our world into a tailspin. Needless to say, he was very angry. He was especially angry at her for ruining his life.

Hold on! Time out. Didn't he have something to do with the demise of the relationship? Did it make him feel good to feel victimized?

After talking about it, he realized that his story, up to that point, had been about personal rejection. He was feeling victimized by the end of their marriage and wanted to blame his ex-wife. His pattern up to that point had been to choose women who were critical of him and emotionally unavailable. We worked on reframing this story and changing it to a story of gratitude, positivity, and personal empowerment. He realized that as long as he was stuck resenting his ex-wife, he would be stuck repeating the same pattern with the next woman he dated. He meditated and focused on bringing in a loving woman. Shortly after, he met a wonderful, supportive partner. Changing the old victim paradigm for a new supportive, loving paradigm, really worked. Hallelujah!

WHAT FEELS GOOD?

What habits do you include in your life that feel good?

What other habits do you want to include in your life that feel good? Think about some positive habits that you would like to include in your life, write them down, and start putting them into action!

For me, exercise is a positive habit that I cannot live without. I love the beautiful, clean air in Santa Fe and I hike as often as possible.

Sometimes I like to hike with a friend, and sometimes I like the solitude of hiking alone.

I also love yoga, meditation, and reading spiritual teachers. Yoga and reading were relatively easy habits for me to embrace. Meditation was much more challenging. I have a very active mind and it took years for me to look forward to sitting still and quieting my mind.

These are just a few examples of positive habits. The bottom line is that a positive habit is one that should make you feel better about yourself. If you feel better about yourself, many aspects of your life will naturally improve.

As you begin, remember to practice non-judgment and acceptance. Be kind to yourself. Try not to be annoyed or frustrated by all the things that you haven't done. Try to focus on what you have done and what you really want to do that feels good. That seems very easy to say, but it is far more difficult to practice. I will discuss this in more detail later in the book.

Remember: Take a deep breath and enjoy the process.

CHAPTER FOUR

PRACTICE BEING PRESENT

Before we continue, think about the title of this chapter. Think about each word separately.

Practice. The exercises in this book, as with most of our life experiences, improve with practice. We don't start out being an expert in anything. It takes time and practice.

Being. Being can simply be understood as existing or as a state of conscious awareness. Throughout this book, think of the act of being as a state of conscious awareness.

Present. Be here in this place with yourself at this moment.

If your life is like mine, it is a luxury to focus only on yourself! Enjoy this opportunity. Being present involves self-observation. It is a "me" moment. This book is filled with "me" moments.

The easiest way to practice being present and to experience a "me" moment is to take a deep breath. Taking a deep breath helps center and focus you in your body. Have you ever noticed how much time you spend in your mind with your thoughts while you ignore the rest of your body, especially your breath?

So, for starters, take a moment and try to be present. Choose any time that works during the course of the day, whenever you are able. Take a minute. Take a break.

1. Take a deep breath.
2. Feel yourself in your body.
3. Ask yourself, "Where am I?" This may seem like an obvious question. But think of it holistically. Where are you with your

mind? Heart? Body? How do you feel at this moment? What are you thinking about? What's going on with you?

Pay attention to as many details as possible.

1. Now take another deep breath.
2. Try to feel yourself in your body. How does your body feel? Is there any difference this time?
3. Next, try to open your heart. What does it mean for you to open your heart? How does that feel? For me, opening my heart is a reminder to feel love and compassion, and that feels really good.

The irony is that although this may begin as a "me" moment, it actually has the potential to turn into an expansive moment. If you are able to focus on your heart, you may be able to get in touch with a greater sense of universal, unconditional love. This may not happen every time, but when it does, it is a transcendental moment.

The Dalai Lama says that the art of happiness is composed of the following feelings: warmth, kindness, and compassion. These emotions are the natural outflow when you open your heart. Gratitude and a positive attitude are soon to follow.

An important aspect of being present is paying attention to your body. Do you have any aches or pains? Is your skin dry? Are you thirsty? Are you too hot or too cold? Is your jaw clenched?

Remember to treat your body royally. This can be as simple as taking a hot bath or shower… or sipping a cup of hot tea or cocoa…or putting lotion on your body…or taking a deep breath.

So, take a deep breath or two or three and enjoy!

CHAPTER FIVE

OBSERVE

For a few days, simply observe yourself. As much as possible, practice self-acceptance and non-judgment. Throughout any given day we all do things that make us feel good and things that make us feel less good. Paying attention is the beginning of it all.

What kinds of actions encourage a sense of well-being? What actions produce a sense of feeling bad?

Do you have certain thoughts that you repeat over and over during the course of a day? Do you have certain moods at specific times during the day? Does your energy level change at different times? Are you more alert in the morning, evening, or afternoon?

Try to document your observations during the course of a day. It is a great way to keep track of your process. If you say or do something you feel good about, make a note of it. If you say or do something you feel bad about, make a note of that as well. Remember to practice non-judgment and self-acceptance throughout this process.

What exactly does it mean to practice non-judgment and self-acceptance? The best way that I can explain this is to think of yourself as a reporter of your thoughts, actions, and behavior. If you were a reporter and were asked to report only the facts about your thoughts, actions, and behavior, how would you report factually about this, without opinion or commentary?

Remember that this is probably a new way to view yourself. We are all students of life. We learn as we go. We learn as we practice.

Negative thoughts will most probably surface at various times. We all have negative thoughts. That is fine and natural. Allow those thoughts to drift by with non-judgment and self-acceptance.

Whenever possible, have a sense of humor about all of this. Try to keep it lighthearted. Make a funny face at yourself in the mirror to loosen up. Practice smiling or laughing at yourself.

Remember throughout all of this to **have fun and feel good**.

And take a deep breath.

CHAPTER SIX

WAKE UP

What's the first thing you do to start your day? You wake up. Take a moment to think about how you feel when you wake up. "Wake up" is a call to action. What does it mean for you to truly wake up? Do you go through your day mechanically? Imagine feeling good, feeling present regardless of what you are doing. We all have challenges in our lives: annoying people, aggravating tasks, financial concerns, health issues. What would you have to change in order to reframe frustration into joy? A lot of it is attitude. Let's start to wake up with an attitude of gratitude!

Read on. The Five Easy Steps are explained on the following pages.

But first, **take a deep breath**.

CHAPTER SEVEN

INTRODUCTION TO THE FIVE EASY STEPS

All you need is five minutes in the morning before you start your day.

Feel free to stay in bed. Remember that this is all about feeling good, so enjoy the luxury of an extra five minutes in bed. If you like, you can glance at the clock when you start and then notice the time when you finish. Even though this is unnecessary, it may be a good gauge for you. You may be surprised at how quickly five minutes go by.

Here are the Five Easy Steps to a happier, more positive, more grateful you.

At least at the beginning, practice the Five Easy Steps while lying in bed. Later, you can do them wherever and whenever the opportunity arises.

If some mornings are too hectic and you can't imagine spending an extra five minutes in bed because you have too much to do, then try practicing the Five Easy Steps at the end of the day before you go to sleep.

The important thing is to keep it simple and to enjoy!

CHAPTER EIGHT

STEP ONE: PAY ATTENTION TO YOUR BREATH

The first thing after you wake up, while lying in bed: **Simply pay attention to your breath.**

What is your breathing like when you first wake up? Do you take short, rapid breaths? Slower, longer breaths? It doesn't really matter. The point is to start to pay attention to your breath. Do this for as long as you like. Even one minute is enough. Simply pay attention to your breathing. Feel free to keep your eyes closed while paying attention to your breath. It may help to focus.

It is best if you are able to wake up without an alarm clock. If you must use an alarm clock, try to wake up to a soothing sound, like a favorite song or a gentle sound, rather than a harsh buzzer. Over time, you can train yourself to wake up without an alarm if you want.* I understand that it isn't always possible, but I highly recommend waking up without an alarm. This way, you start your day with a sense of empowerment because you are choosing how and when to wake up rather than relying on an external source.

* I mentioned this in Chapter Two as well. After you've been doing this practice for a while, you may want to train yourself to wake up without an alarm clock. It is easier than you think to wake up without an alarm clock. Before you go to bed, tell yourself the time that you would like to wake up. You can say it out loud, write it down, or just think about it. Go to sleep and see what happens. The first few times you do this, you may wake up several times just to make sure you don't oversleep. You can always set your alarm clock as a

backup so that you don't have to worry about oversleeping.

For now, simply pay attention to your breath when you wake up.

CHAPTER NINE

STEP TWO: CONSCIOUSLY TAKE A DEEP BREATH

It is helpful to keep your eyes gently closed for this exercise. If you keep your eyes closed, focus your gaze on your third eye, the eye of inner knowing, which is located between and slightly above your eyebrows (approximately one-half to one inch above). Remember to keep your eyes and eyelids relaxed when closed.

First, just take one deep breath. Try to inhale slowly into your belly and exhale slowly. Once you have done that, start a rhythmic type of breathing. Inhale to the count of four. Hold your breath to the count of four. Exhale to the count of four. You can count to whatever number you please. The important thing is to count evenly for the inhale, the hold, and the exhale. Repeat this at least four times.

This is a simple form of meditation. Without consciously thinking about it, you have simplified your thought process by focusing on your breath.

Reminder: These are guidelines. Feel free to take more than four deep breaths. Four times, for me, was a good start.

How are you feeling? Pay attention to how you feel after a few slow, deep breaths.

Please note that this breathing technique is excellent for reducing anxiety as well. If you feel anxious or nervous during the day, try following this rhythmic breathing and see if it helps.

CHAPTER TEN

STEP THREE: PRACTICE GRATITUDE

Now think of three things that you are grateful for.

It can be as simple as the fact that you are grateful for an extra five minutes in bed. Or you are grateful for your bed. Or you are grateful for electricity. Or hot water. Or sunshine. There is no need to feel like you have to come up with something profound. A simple thought of gratitude is perfect. If it helps, keep a notepad, a piece of paper, or a techno-gadget nearby to write it down. You may find this useful later on down the road. Even if you write down just one reason to be grateful each day for thirty days, you will have a list of thirty things that you are grateful for in one month and 365 things you are grateful for in one year. You will also find that the more you do this, the easier it becomes.

When I started my gratefuloptimism.com website, I made a one-year commitment to post daily affirmations on it. I experienced some fear. I was especially fearful that I wouldn't be able to think of enough affirmations. What if I couldn't think of one for each day? What if people thought the affirmations were silly? What if people thought they were superficial? I was afraid of being judged. At first, the challenge seemed daunting. In spite of my fears, I stuck to it. Once I got into the habit, it became easier and easier. After a couple of months, I looked forward to this practice. Now I reread the affirmations and feel a sense of pride and gratitude for my accomplishment.

And…take a deep breath.

CHAPTER ELEVEN

STEP FOUR: SET YOUR INTENTION FOR THE DAY

Before getting out of bed, spend a minute thinking about your day and set the intention for the kind of day you would like to experience.

When setting an intention, it is very important to state it in the affirmative. Focus on what you want rather than what you don't want. That way, you are setting a positive tone for your intention instead of a negative one.

A good guideline is that if the intention includes the word "not," it is probably negative. An example of a negative intention might be: My intention for today is that I'm not going to lose my temper. The positive version of this intention would be: My intention for today is to remain calm in all situations.

When setting your intention, try speaking the intention out loud. This brings additional energy and vitality to the intention. You may want to write it down and keep it with you as a reminder during the day.

Some examples for setting your positive intention for the day are:

My intention for today is to keep a positive attitude in all situations.

My intention for today is to send positive energy to all people whom I encounter.

My intention for today is to accept the natural flow of the day.

My intention for today is to practice self-acceptance.

My intention for today is to practice non-judgment.

My intention for today is to feel more compassion toward others.

My intention for today is to laugh more.

My intention for today is to be patient with myself and others.

My intention for today is to remember to notice the beauty that surrounds me.

My intention for today is to focus on my breath as often as possible.

After employing the practice of setting your intention for each day for several days, you may decide to take this a step further and begin to proactively plan and strategize about your day. This may be challenging. If it is, simply read through the suggestions mentioned below and wait until you feel like you are ready to tackle this one.

Start by thinking: "What do I need to do today? Is there anything happening during the day that I am concerned about?" If there is something difficult, try to think about how you might be able to approach a challenge differently that might improve the situation.

For example, you may have to interact with a difficult person at your place of work during the day. We all know who those people are! They always seem to say the wrong thing at the wrong time. You usually feel a sense of apprehension beforehand, because you know that the interaction may be unpleasant. Let's see how we can turn this situation around.

First, try to send that person positive energy. Think of one thing about that person that you like or one thing that you might have in common. It may be appreciation of family or a pet or a piece of jewelry or clothing. When

I worked in the corporate world, there were difficult people with large egos and arrogant attitudes. There was one person in particular who did not operate from a place of integrity. I found him to be untrustworthy and I dreaded interacting with him. One time, I asked him about the photo of his family on his desk. He told me a little about them. It was clear how much he loved his wife and children. I realized that he was proud of his family in the same way that I am proud of my family. While I never looked forward to interacting with him, I had found a commonality between us. This discovery was helpful for me when working with him and I found it easier to send positive energy his way.

Sometimes it is very challenging to send positive energy to a difficult person. If that is the case, then try to find a way to think of that person compassionately. If the person is angry or combative, think of how much negative energy he or she is carrying around inside and what a challenge that must be. Most probably that person operates from a place of fear (as mentioned in the Preface). Send thoughts of peace and serenity.

Another technique is to keep helpful sayings readily visible, like the Serenity Prayer written by Reinhold Niebuhr and used by Alcoholics Anonymous. It says: "God grant me serenity to accept the things I cannot change, courage to change the things I can, and the wisdom to know the difference." There is a great amount of wisdom in this prayer. We are often confronted with situations that are not ideal. This prayer serves as a wonderful reminder and helps keep a healthy perspective during trying moments.

The Four Agreements by Don Miguel Ruiz is a wonderful book that has also helped me a great deal.

The Four Agreements are:
"Be impeccable with your word.
Don't make assumptions.
Don't take anything personally.
Always do your best."

This book is easy to read and a great reference. I have shared these agreements with my friends and colleagues and it has really helped us cope with daily challenges.

Once you have some coping strategies, it makes even the most challenging situations a little easier.

In addition, think of something you are looking forward to during the day: maybe lunch with a friend, a wonderful cup of coffee, connecting with someone important to you, a good book you want to read, a walk in the park, etc.

Send yourself good thoughts and blessings for the day.

And...**take a deep breath.**

CHAPTER TWELVE

STEP FIVE:
SAY A KIND WORD

Decide to say a kind word to or do one kind thing for one person during the day. As a matter of fact, say one kind thing to the first person you see. Why not start by saying one kind thing to yourself?

You can thank yourself for always trying to do your best. You can thank yourself for preparing a great meal or making a fabulous cup of coffee or tea. You can thank someone else for an act of kindness. You can compliment someone's outfit. You can open the door for someone. You can let a car into your lane during traffic. You can give someone a nice smile.

Thank yourself for taking a deep breath!

CHAPTER THIRTEEN

SUMMARY OF THE FIVE EASY STEPS

The Five Easy Steps are:

Step One: Pay Attention to Your Breath

Step Two: Consciously Take a Deep Breath

Step Three: Practice Gratitude

Step Four: Set Your Intention for the Day

Step Five: Say a Kind Word

That's it. You're ready to start your day.

For starters, try this for seven days. One week. Five minutes each morning. If it feels good, continue this practice until it becomes a habit, which usually takes a minimum of three weeks.

This is the basic outline. Now let's discuss what happens next.

And feel free to take another **deep breath!**

CHAPTER FOURTEEN
FORGIVENESS

As you go through the Five Steps, doubts may arise. Perhaps it feels too hard, or you can't concentrate, or you lose focus, or you may forget to practice the Five Easy Steps one morning. It's no big deal. *Accept* that you couldn't focus or that you forgot. Life sometimes gets in the way. It happens.

Of course, we have all committed worse transgressions than forgetting to practice the Five Easy Steps! After all, we are human and by our very nature imperfect. We are bound to make mistakes. Regardless of the magnitude of the mistake, true forgiveness can free us from bad feelings we are holding on to about ourselves or others. Accept that a mistake was made, let go, and move on.

Forgiveness is an act of kindness we do for ourselves. Forgiveness is *letting go* of negative feelings toward oneself or another person. It is one of the greatest gifts we can bestow upon ourselves.

When we are unable to forgive, we hold on to strong negative emotions such as guilt, shame, resentment, or anger. These emotions not only feel bad, they may adversely affect our health. Conversely, when we are able to forgive, a tremendous weight is lifted from our psyche. We feel so much better when we forgive.

What do you need to do in order to forgive? Start by observing yourself. When you think of forgiving yourself or someone else, is there a place in your body where you feel discomfort? How does it feel? Does it feel like butterflies in your stomach? Does it feel like a headache? Does it feel like tightness in your chest? Do you feel a strong emotion? Do you feel anxious? Do you feel angry? Do you feel ashamed? Do you feel guilty? These would all be considered "bad" feelings.

Any time you feel nervous, sad, angry, or any kind of bad feeling, the first step is always just to **take a deep breath**.

It sounds easy, but getting out of your mind can be very challenging. Reread Chapter Four and practice being present. First of all, remember the word "practice." This is all about practicing. Then remember the idea of being present.

Practice being here, with yourself, in this moment, by taking a deep breath.

It always starts by focusing on your breath. Your breath will naturally deepen over time. The only thing you need to remember is to take a deep breath…one breath at a time.

Try to be an objective, nonjudgmental observer of yourself. If you can practice non-judgment with yourself, you will find it easier to practice non-judgment with others also.

What does non-judgment mean for you? For me, it is about *accepting* the present as it is, and the past as it was, without adding opinions like, "I'm a bad person," or "I'm ashamed," or "I'm so stupid."

A nonjudgmental approach would be, "I made a mistake. I did something that I feel bad about. It's all right. I'm human. I make mistakes. I understand. First, let me focus on my breath, one breath at a time. I just need to pay attention to my breath. One breath. Inhale. Exhale."

As you focus on your breath, you may want to close your eyes and focus on your third eye. Allow yourself to release the anger, resentment, shame, etc. Say to yourself, "I forgive myself." (You can replace "myself" with the name of a person whom you want to forgive.) I am ready to let go of these feelings of _____. (Fill in the blank with whatever negative feelings you choose.) If you like, repeat this several times until you truly feel a sense of forgiveness and letting go.

Forgiveness is not easy but it is truly liberating. As Alexander Pope so beautifully stated: "To err is human, to forgive divine." Feel your own moment of divine consciousness and forgive.

Remember to practice kindness and compassion with yourself as well, and...

If you can only practice one step, then let it be to take a deep breath or two or three.

CHAPTER FIFTEEN

AFFIRMATIONS

Affirmations are an essential part of my daily practice. An affirmation is a positive statement of encouragement and support. It plants the seeds for success in our lives. Affirmations should be stated in the present tense and in the affirmative. This helps us feel that the affirmation is already a reality, rather than a distant hope or far-off dream. Stating it in the affirmative focuses on what we *want* rather than what we don't want.

There has been a lot written about using the present tense of the verb "to be" when talking about ourselves. Deepak Chopra and Wayne Dyer have written and spoken about this. Tom Shadyack also discussed it in his movie, "*I Am.*"

"I am" is a reference to the divine within each of us. It is mentioned in the Old Testament, In Exodus 3:14, Moses asks God what to call God when Moses speaks of God to the Israelites. God says, "I Am That I Am." God goes on to say: "You shall tell the Israelites that 'I am' [God] sent me [Moses] to you [the Israelites]."

This is a very important concept. If you remember that every time you utter the words "I am" you are speaking about your own divinity, you will realize the power of these words.

Affirmations are an excellent way to remind ourselves of the divine within each and every one of us. Affirmations always help us to remind ourselves of the reality, wishes, and dreams we want for ourselves, our loved ones, and the world.

Some examples of simple affirmations are:

I am happy.
I am abundant.

I am loved.
I am beautiful.
I am successful.
I am healthy.
I am loving.
I am patient.
I am peaceful.
I am content.
I am joyful.
I am grateful.
I am talented.
I am powerful.
I am capable.
I am spiritual.

These affirmations may be expanded upon, as well. For example, I am grateful can be expanded by saying: I am grateful for...this beautiful day, a good night's sleep, my comfortable bed...

We can create our own affirmations to provide strength and encouragement in our daily lives.

Neville Goddard, a metaphysical thinker of the twentieth century, talks about living from the wish fulfilled. This means to speak and act as if whatever you want is already part of your life. Affirmations are a wonderful way to practice this.

If you need help thinking of affirmations that resonate with you, just use the Internet and search for affirmations. The Internet is an abundant resource.

And, as always, **take a deep breath**.

CHAPTER SIXTEEN

LAUGH

Always remember to laugh. Laughter has many benefits. You've all heard the saying, "Laughter is the best medicine." It is true. There are scientific studies to support this. In 2011, I became a Laughter Yoga teacher and trainer. Studying and practicing Laughter Yoga has been a wonderful experience.

Go to www.youtube.com and search for Laughter Yoga. There are hundreds of videos. Some of them will make you laugh. Have you ever noticed that laughter is contagious? Have you ever noticed that you can't feel bad when you are laughing?

That's because the many benefits of laughter include:

- Reduced stress
- Lowered blood pressure
- Boosted immune system
- Reduced pain
- Improved breathing
- Relaxed muscles

Laughter Yoga is based on these five principles:

- Laughter Yoga is unique. Anyone can laugh for no reason.
- We initiate laughter as an exercise, but with eye contact and childlike playfulness it turns into real and contagious laughter.
- It is called Laughter Yoga because it combines laughter exercises with yoga breathing, which brings oxygen to the body and brain and makes us feel more energetic.
- It is based on the scientific fact that the body cannot differentiate between real and fake laughter. We reap the same benefits.
- It was started by a medical doctor, Dr. Madan Kataria, in 1995 in a park in Mumbai, India with five people. Now

there are thousands of laughter clubs in more than seventy countries.

If you are interested in learning more about Laughter Yoga, visit my website www.gratefuloptimism.com or www.laughteryoga.org.

In any event, the most important thing is to **remember to laugh**.

You naturally have to take a deep breath when you laugh.

Doesn't that feel wonderful?

CHAPTER SEVENTEEN

NEXT STEPS

What do you do after you have followed the Five Easy Steps for three weeks? If you are feeling better and would like to take your "practice" to the next level, here are a few suggestions:

1. ADD TO YOUR PRACTICE

Increase the amount of time you spend practicing in the morning. Take four more deep breaths. Write down one or two additional things you are grateful for. Think of more opportunities to say nice things to people.

Increase the frequency. For example, increase the number of times you practice during the day. Try adding a practice before you go to sleep, perhaps while you are lying in bed.

Instead of saying a kind word to one person, say a kind word to two people, and then say a kind word to yourself.

Practice at opportune moments throughout the day: more breaths, more thoughts of gratitude, more kind words, more mindfulness, more times during the day.

2. REFINE YOUR PRACTICE

Think about how your practice has been evolving. Are you enjoying it? Do you feel better? Would you like to take more deep breaths? Would you like to find more opportunities to say kind words? Would you like to include more acts of kindness?

3. MODIFY YOUR PRACTICE

Is there anything that you would like to do differently? Remember that this practice is to help you feel better. What aspects of the practice make you feel good? Perhaps you would like to add a moment to think about what you are looking forward to during the day.

Perhaps you would like to write more things down. Perhaps you would like to spend more time breathing.

4. CONTINUE YOUR PRACTICE

Do you want to make these easy steps part of your daily habit? Does it feel good? The more you do it, the easier it becomes.

5. REVIEW

Ask yourself some questions:

- What helps?
- What do you like the most?
- What feels good?
- What feels bad?
- Do I feel more positive?
- Do I feel more grateful?
- Do I feel good more often?
- Am I more present in the current moment?
- Am I handling difficult situations with more ease?
- Do I feel happier?

- Does it feel good to pay attention to my breath?
- Does paying attention to my breath help me focus?
- Does it help me feel more centered?

How does it feel when you take a deep breath?

If it feels good, **take a few deep breaths** before continuing.

CHAPTER EIGHTEEN

FOOD FOR THOUGHT

What is a state of grace? For me, a state of grace is a holistic moment. It is a moment when I have felt a connection with the divine within me and others. There is a purity of being at those moments.

One such time for me was on 11/11/11 at 11:00 a.m. You may be aware that the number eleven represents connecting lines of heaven and earth. Earlier in the book, I mentioned the nonprofit that I am involved with called Unicopia. Our inaugural event for Unicopia was on 11/11/11. We held a summit that day with about fifty participants. At 11:00 a.m., we took a moment to: "Visualize the community and the world as you want it to be. Open your hearts and imagine a sustainable future for yourself, your family, and the world." It was a powerful moment when I experienced a profound sense of love and unity: with the divine, with the community, with the planet, with all life.

Have you experienced a state of grace? What were the circumstances? What was it like? How did you feel? You might want to write it down as a reminder for when you aren't feeling that way. Feel free to post it on my blog as well.

Here are some deeper questions to ask yourself:

- Do you consider yourself generally optimistic or pessimistic? Why?
- What percentage of the time do you feel good? Bad?
- Is there a certain time of day that you feel good? Bad?
- What things do you do that make you feel good?

- Do you have a feel-good friend? A friend who helps you feel better and helps you laugh?
- Do you have a feel-good tree or flower or plant? A tree or flower or plant that makes you feel better every time you see it?
- Do you have a feel-good movie that you watch? A movie that makes you feel better when you watch it?
- Do you have a feel-good song? A song that you love hearing or singing along with?
- Do you have a feel-good artist? An artist whose work makes you feel good every time you see it?
- Do you have a feel-good restaurant?
- Do you have a feel-good food?
- How do your feelings, attitudes, and energy affect planetary health?

It is important to remember that we are all connected. Unity consciousness is the interconnectedness of all things.

What comes out of experiencing unity consciousness? For me, love, compassion, joy, kindness, and peace of mind which lead ultimately to a state of grace.

Choose love. Choose joy. Choose gratitude.

Feel good and take a deep breath.

APPENDIX: RESOURCES

These are a few of my favorites. The world is your oyster. Enjoy!

FILMS

It's a Wonderful Life
The Wizard of Oz
The Sound of Music
Forrest Gump
Singin' in the Rain
E.T.
The Princess Bride
Mary Poppins
Babe
Beauty and the Beast (Disney)
Modern Times
Legally Blonde
My Cousin Vinny
Midnight in Paris
Rio

The Artist
Gandhi
I Am
Searching for Sugarman
Jane's Journey
Buck

WEBSITES
Deepak Chopra:
www.deepakchopra.com
Oprah: www.oprah.com
Silva: www.silvamethod.com
Yogananda: www.yogananda-srf.org
Wayne Dyer: www.drwaynedyer.com
Hay House: www.hayhouse.com
Dalai Lama: www.dalailama.com
Dr. Dan Siegel: www.drdansiegel.com
Science of Mind:
www.scienceofmind.com
Laughter yoga: www.laughteryoga.org
Grateful Optimism: www.gratefuloptimism.com
Unicopia: www.unicopia.org

BOOKS

Dalai Lama: *The Art of Happiness*
Deepak Chopra: *The Seven Spiritual Laws of Success*
Wayne Dyer: *Wishes Fulfilled*
Eckhart Tolle: *The Power of Now*
Shakti Gawain: *Creative Visualization*
Paramahansa Yogananda: *Autobiography of a Yogi*
Thich Nhat Hanh: *Peace Is Every Step*
Jon Kabat-Zinn: *Wherever You Go There You Are*
Don Miguel Ruiz: *The Four Agreements*
Rhonda Byrne: *The Secret*
Neville Goddard: *The Power of Awareness*
Lao-Tzu: *Tao Te Ching*
Rumi: *The Essential Rumi*
Thomas More: *Utopia*
Anita Moorjani: *Dying to Be Me*
Elizabeth Gilbert: *Eat, Pray, Love*

MUSIC

Classical music
Jazz
Latin music
Rock and roll

Folk music
Rhythm and blues
Hip-hop
Country
Instrumental
Spiritual

ARTISTS
Michelangelo
Da Vinci
Rembrandt
Botticelli
Monet
Renoir
Bonnard
Lautrec
Gauguin
Picasso
Rousseau
O'Keeffe
Rothko

ABOUT THE AUTHOR:

Maxine Swisa is an accomplished author, educator, and innovator who has taught classes, led tours, conducted seminars, participated in public speaking engagements, radio shows, and panel discussions, and contributed to a book on executive leadership. She is a laughter yoga instructor and trainer as well as an ESOL (English for Speakers of Other Languages) teacher.

After retiring from a career in Information Technology, Swisa partnered with a builder, designer and visionary to create the award-winning, zero-energy Emerald Home in Santa Fe, New Mexico. This partnership led to the re-emergence of Unicopia, www.unicopia.org, a nonprofit organization dedicated to cultivating the awareness, knowledge, and synergy that is essential for our sustainable future.

An eternal optimist, Ms. Swisa shares daily affirmations of gratitude on her website, www.gratefuloptimism.com.

Ms. Swisa believes her most important achievement to date has been raising her two beautiful daughters, Maya and Adi.

CONTACT INFORMATION:

If you have any questions or comments, email me at maxine@greenbackpublishing.com. I would love to hear from you. Please feel free to write on my blog:
http://www.gratefuloptimism.blogspot.com/

Learn more about our nonprofit:
www.unicopia.org

Enjoy daily affirmations of gratitude at
www.gratefuloptimism.com

Visit our publishing website:
www.greenbackpublishing.com

Notes

Notes

Notes

Notes

Notes

Notes

Notes

Notes

Notes